AF433622

DEVOTIONS
In The Wind
•RIDING FOR JESUS•

*This work is dedicated to
all Brothers and Sisters
who ride. To those who
know Jesus, and those who
have yet to meet Him.*

Contents

Introduction

"My heart rejoices in the Eternal One; my strength grows strong in the Lord. My mouth can mock my enemies because I celebrate how You have saved me!"
1 Sam 2:1 NLT

Riding motorcycles has been a passion for most of my life. I still remember the thrill of learning to ride my first bike in 1982 - a 1965 BSA Lighting. I traded my first car, which was a 1955 classic Olds, straight across for the chopped out, kick start British bike.

So there I was, with the shiny new bike sitting in my garage, and I had no clue even how to start it, much less how to ride it! It was the beginning of many fun years of riding, but it also took me down some dark roads.

The outlaw motorcycle world I found myself in eventually led me to a very hard place. But sometimes it's in those places of desperation, that people find Jesus. I was radically saved, and gave up riding to follow my Lord, get married and raise a child. It was so worth it, but after sending my daughter off to college, I asked the Lord if I could have my motorcycle back. He said yes!.. which has led to the best riding of my life over the last 18 years.

I've made so many friends related to riding… but there's something special about my Christian brothers & sisters who ride. We share a camaraderie at a deeper level than the typical biker culture. Sharing the 'blood covenant' relationship with our Lord Jesus, sets us apart from the rest of the world, and is an undeniable bond. This book is written for you.

We, dear brothers & sisters are in a unique position to reach the biker world for Christ. We can be His hands and feet and voice. So even though this was written with many themes to strengthen you in your walk with God, my main goal is to encourage you in being a person God can use in the motorcycle culture. Be the light. We may be the only church some of them will ever know.

If you're like me, you remember the days when you wouldn't set foot in a church, and had no time for Jesus freaks. But I know that if God can turn you & me around, there's hope for even the worst case biker. There is no one that is too far gone that He can't reach.

Someone recently said he thinks of me like his 'Biker Mom' figure. I like that. Will you let me be your 'Biker Mom' for a few days?

We Can't Explain it...

Psalm 34:8 TPT
Taste and see that the Lord is good. Oh, the
joys of those who take refuge in him!

There is real freedom in riding motorcycles. I love the open road, the wind in my face, the solitude of the adventure. Those who ride experience something that moves the soul in ways that a non-rider just can't understand.

In many ways, the same thing can be said about our relationship with the living God. The freedom of being right with God gives us a joy and a comfort that settles deep in our souls. It's not something you can explain. Knowing God is one of those things that can't really be understood until you experience it for yourself.

Some riders may not understand, but they're watching. We cannot forget that. Whether or not we want to share our faith, if people know you're a believer, they are watching and judging. So be real, and be authentic. Not 'holier than thou', but someone who is confident in their faith, and not afraid to say so.

Of course, this assumes they do know you're a believer. I remember one time thinking "Do my co-workers know I'm a Christian?" I felt it was a sad testimony that most of them at that time probably didn't. I know there's not a lot of opportunity to talk about our faith in the work place, but there are many ways we can - and should - make it obvious where we're coming from. Our lives and attitude should speak volumes about whether we are in the 'world' or followers of Christ. You might think, "I can't explain it… they won't understand." Listen, I'm not talking about evangelizing. So how do we share our faith authentically? Here's a few stories to explain.

My husband & I are part of the local riding club, and hang out with them a lot. We were at a meeting where they were going over the ride schedule, and my husband said, 'Darn! That lake ride is on a Sunday, and we won't be able to make it because we go to church on Sundays." This statement says that church is a priority.

When we are meeting for a group ride, my husband or I will ask if anyone minds if we say a 'road prayer' before taking off. We have yet to have anyone say we can't do it. Another way to do this, is to say "We are having a little road prayer over here if anyone wants to join us."

As bikers hang out and talk, a conversation might come up about a family sickness or tragedy. We can offer to pray for them or that situation. If it's possible, pull the person aside and pray with them right then. If that's not possible, you might just tell them that you will be praying for that situation. Most people appreciate that.

The simple way to think about this, is to **be yourself, and don't hide your faith.**

Prayer focus: Lord, help me to be natural and authentic in sharing my faith. Amen.

Wind Therapy

Psalm 17:6 TPT
You will answer me, God; I know you always will, like you always
do as you listen with love to my every prayer.

Sometimes riding by yourself down a country road is just the therapy we need after a hard day or week. The pressures blow off us with the wind, our mind is freed, and we breath in the fresh air. It's where the stress of the day or week can be drowned out by the road when all we have to think about is how to lean into the next turn.

It's one of my favorite times to meet with God to talk about things that are on my mind. The freedom to talk with God at any time, any where is always there, and it's a comfort. But there is something special about my prayers in the 'saddle'. It can't get more private than this. Just me and God and the road.

Prayer is essential when doing motorcycle ministry. Whether you're part of a ministry group, Christian motorcycle club or just a lone Christian rider, it's the primary way we prepare for the opportunities that come when we are out on the road on our bikes. We want to build ourselves up in prayer before going out into the mission field.

We also want to be comfortable praying out loud for those He puts in our path. A good practice is to ask for permission to pray for people. It respects their space, and it's rare to have anyone say no when I've asked if I can pray for them. If the person has a personal need, you may want to take them aside to have a more private prayer time, or pray quietly with them. Most people want prayer but don't want to be embarrassed in front of others, so this helps them be a little more comfortable to open up to receive what God has for them.

If there are other brothers/sisters of faith with you, inviting a prayer circle may be the right move too. Try to sense the comfort level of the person you are praying for.

Recently I was on a group ride with some people from my church, and my friend asked the waitress if she had any prayer needs. At first she was hesitant and didn't really have anything in mind for prayer. My friend offered to just bless her in her job and finances. Then she perked up and said, "Yes, things have been tough financially for me lately." So the 5 of us in the booth proceeded to pronounce God's blessings over her family and her finances. She was so appreciative, and you could see she walked away with a bit of joy and hope. I share this story to illustrate that God may use you to minister to anyone when you're out on the road… it may not be another biker!

Prayer Focus: Father, I am available to be your instrument to touch others with your love.

The Journey

Psalm 25:4 TPT
Lord, direct me throughout my journey so I can experience your plans for my life. Reveal the life-paths that are pleasing to you.

We love every journey on our motorcycles. It doesn't matter if there's a destination in mind, or we're just following the front wheel. Just being in the wind is enough.

Our journey with God is not so random though. He has a plan and purpose for our world, and especially for His people. We are part of something much bigger than this world, but have our part to play in it. Life is a journey of learning each day who we really are in Christ, and what our part is.

Sometimes we struggle trying to fit into the 'world' and its ways. We do live in the world, and are part of it, but we must remember that our purpose is not to fit into this world. We have a higher calling. Our Father made each of us to be the unique person that we are, and we have our own unique part to play in His plan. The best way we can fulfill that purpose, is to be the unique person He made us to be! We don't have to try to be what anyone else wants us to be or expects us to be. We don't have to apologize for who we are or aren't. We are God's masterpiece, and He loves us for exactly who we are.

Have you considered your love for motorcycles is the tool He wants to use to reach other motorcycle riders through you?

We are uniquely positioned to reach this specific people group. When we give our gifts to Him as a sacrifice of service, He will open doors of opportunities for us to use that gift for His purposes. What an amazing blessing and honor to serve the most high King with our motorcycle!

"Whatever you do, work at it with all your heart, as working for the Lord, not for human masters, since you know that you will receive an inheritance from the Lord as a reward. It is the Lord Christ you are serving." Colossians 3:23-24 NIV

Let's not take this responsibility too lightly. Yes, we love riding and the wind in our face - that's who we are, and our motorcycle is the gift we bring to God's altar. So let's rejoice in our calling and **ride for the King**!

Prayer focus: Father, direct me on my life journey so I can experience your plans and purpose for me. Reveal the life paths that are pleasing to you.

The Long View

Joshua 1:9
Be strong and courageous. Do not be afraid or discouraged, for the Lord your God is with you where ever you go.

Some of the best views are the ones you get to via a long twisty road on a motorcycle. Half the fun is getting there, and it makes the time you get to sit and enjoy the view even richer.

One of the most beautiful rides I've enjoyed with long views was the Skyline Hwy in the Smokey Mountains. The road goes along the mountain tops with stunning views of the hills and valleys with beautiful lakes, streams and green pastures along the way. There is something peaceful and restful in being out in God's creation and taking a moment to soak in all its beauty. It "restores my soul".

We don't always get a 'long view' ahead in our journey through this life though. It's the mystery of what's ahead that gives us hope and faith for the things unseen. It's easy to get caught up in our every day grind and become overwhelmed and stressed. But when we turn our thoughts back to God, we can pause, take a deep breath and remember that life is short, but we have eternity ahead. We can trust Him to guide us along life paths, and remember that His yoke is easy.

If life seems too hard, we need to recalibrate our thinking.

Psalm 23 is a passage I come back to again and again to find that calming place where the Lord, my Shepherd is leading me beside still waters and green pastures. Kind of like those beautiful places we get to riding down twisty roads on our bikes. No wonder there is documented proof that riding a motorcycle is good therapy for stress!

When life gets hard, we can trust God to direct our steps, and our part is to be strong and courageous and not get discouraged. In our spiritual walk, our Father has revealed a 'long view' - His plan that lets us to see way out into eternity. We don't have to worry about what happens after this life, and that gives us a new confidence in how we live out our time here on Earth. He has placed heaven in our hearts, and the thought of eternity is so big, it puts everything else in a new perspective.

The more we recalibrate, the less we have to. It's like we give God's Spirit a larger and larger place to dwell in us. More of Him, and less of us. And people can sense that peace in our spirits. It's what makes them hungry for what we have. The greatest witness we can give is living a God-centered life in front of those who don't know Him.

Prayer Focus: Thank you Lord for the 'long view' and helping me to recalibrate when I need it. May my peace be a beacon of hope for others. Amen.

Shining Like the Sun

Daniel 12:3 NIV
Those who are wise will shine like the brightness of the
heavens, and those who lead many to righteousness,
like the stars for ever and ever..

If you've ridden long enough, you've had the experience of the sun blinding you on the road. For brief moments, we can't see where we're going, and it can bring on an adrenalin rush that feels like a brush with death. But the moment passes and we can see again, and all is right with the world.

There are verses in the Bible that talk about the countenance of God being so bright that people can't even look at Him. And the scripture above says we will shine like the brightness of the heavens when we are wise and lead others to righteousness. Our brightness might even last forever, like a star in the universe! It kind of blows my mind to think about that.

So how do we 'shine' for Jesus and lead others to righteousness? What does that look like? Well, for starters, we love people. Jesus gave us a command to love each other. "**Your love for one another** will prove to the world that you are my disciples." (John 13:34-35 NLT)

Loving on people means we care about them. We go the extra mile for them. In the biker world, it means that if a brother breaks down on the road, we stay with them until help arrives. If they're sick or in the hospital, we visit them. If they're in need, we try to help. It's a command - not a suggestion, which means we have a responsibility! Jesus even went so far as to say that when we refuse to help these brothers & sisters, we were refusing to help Him. That puts a new perspective on helping others, doesn't it?

Of course the ultimate way to love someone is to help them understand their need for Jesus.

This was actually the last command that Jesus left us with. "Go and make disciples." Now that command is a more delicate matter, because unsaved people generally don't want to be beaten over the head with scriptures. It takes time and strategy to develop relationships so that we can speak into their lives.

When they see the love we have for each other, it is the beginning of softening their hearts. We really don't have the power to save anybody… that's what God the Holy Spirit do. If we're available to be used, He will give us the honor of helping to walk another soul into the Kingdom as the Holy Spirit gives life to those He chooses. Maybe our efforts will just plant seeds of knowledge or seeds of hope in their hearts, but this is sometimes the path that leads them to the truth. This is exactly how I found Jesus… through a lot of 'seeds' that acted like bread crumbs leading to my savior.

Prayer Focus: Father, here am I, use me! I want to shine your light into the lives of my brothers and sisters that need to know you. Amen.

Stories From The Road
Lito's Story

Sometimes our walk down the path of our faith consists in various meetings on the road. Let me explain what I mean. When making the choice of starting my own journey, I met someone on the road. In the beginning they started me on the path of following God, eventually sending me on down the road. I laugh now because my ministry is literally on the road.

Just like any journey, you will meet people in various stages and places along the way. When I became a member of the ministry I'm a part of now, I began with a mindset to love and embrace the **"earning the right to be heard"** concept of doing ministry. Accepting people for where they are, and walking alongside of them was truly all I ever longed for. I would see so much fruit from that concept.

Here's an example: In the riding club I belong to, they have a 'no religion' and 'no politics' policy. This meant they did not really want to get involved in those two things, but our old club director warmed up to us (Christians in the group) and allowed a bit of ministry. Most of the members did not really like the fact that we began to pray at certain times here and there. Then as new leadership rose up, we began to be put on the back burner, but it didn't stop us. We continued to be used and served where we could, mostly with one-on-one ministry.

Like the night I prayed for our ex-military director at a "bike night" event. If you knew him, you'd know he generally steered away from us. He accepted us as club members, but that's about as far as it went.

One night I saw him wearing a neck brace and asked him about it. He explained that he had worn it off and on over the years, and now he was once again going to have another surgery on his neck, and this surgery might cause him to wear it indefinitely. So knowing he wasn't big on praying, I just said, "I'll pray for you", and then went on to talk about bikes and the weather. (I did my best to not make a big deal out of praying for him.)

The next time I saw him, it was from a distance, but I noticed he had no neck brace. When we caught eyes, he swished his neck all around showing he had full motion in it. We didn't discuss it, and I didn't followup, but the simple roll of his neck and his lips saying "thank you", was as if the heavens and earth moved for me. To this day he comes to our booth at biker events to show us love and respect.

This is what ministry for me is all about. Sowing seeds and allowing God to bring the harvest. The best way we can do that is 'meetings on the road', meeting people where they are, how they look and how they act. Trying to understand them will give us a greater insight for how we can lead them to God. In order to do that, we need to accept them for who they are in that moment, and look for the open doors to do ministry.

It's always amazing when I get to hit the road to have fellowship and do ministry.... I know most people see my adventures and think, "Man it must be nice to be on vacation every weekend." But only a handful of people know what is truly involved, they don't know about the one on one conversions that happen. They don't know about the breaking of bread, and sharing of life that takes place. They don't see the tears, the hard conversations, or the ministry devoted to others that is needed. But I would not have it any other way, for these are the transformational, heart changing, wound healing parts of life and I wouldn't miss these moments for the world.   -*Lito*

God's Timing

2nd Peter 3:9 NIV
The Lord is not slow in keeping his promise, as some
understand slowness. Instead he is patient with you,
not wanting anyone to perish.

Waiting for the Lord to answer our prayers is always an interesting challenge. Our faith is tested, and then we have all those questions when the answer is 'no'. It always takes me a minute to come back around to simply trusting that my Father knows best or has a plan that may not make sense to me. We know we've matured in our faith when our trust never wavers, even when we don't get what we want.

Waiting patiently just isn't something most of us are good at, but when it has to do with our spiritual growth, we need to remember what scripture says about being 'exceedingly glad' in tests and trials, because it's those experiences that build our character. And this journey with God is all about becoming more & more like Him.

It's that character that gives us the respect and credibility we need when it comes to sharing our faith with other riders.

We sometimes need a lot of patience to wait for the right timing to approach someone about Jesus. Or we may need to throw out a lot of 'seeds' in our circle of influence before they make a difference.

It reminds me of a lady in a riding group I belonged to, who was one tough cookie. She was an ex-cop and body builder with a very strong and independent personality. We got to know each other through the riding club, and she sometimes threw tough spiritual questions at me when the occasion arose - almost as a challenge. It felt like I was really put on trial, but I was extremely patient with the questions and one day she surprised me with a call to ask if she could go to church with me! Trying to hide my shock, I couldn't believe the timing of this request… I was suffering with a bad flu and had to stay home! But I told her to go anyway. I know stepping into a church where you don't know anyone can be intimating. I told her how comfortable and casual the church was and that she would really enjoy the music. I talked about what a great teacher our pastor was. Long story short, I stayed on the phone with her during the whole drive from her home until she got to the church, coaching her about not turning back, and to be the strong woman I knew she was, to follow through with what God was telling her to do. She made it to the church and stuck through the service, and it was a turning point for that lady. **My patience with her had paid off.**

Prayer Focus: Lord, let patience have it's perfect work in me, so I can have patience in others to see your love and plan come to fruition.

Shiny and New

2nd Cor 5:18 TPT
God has made all things new, and reconciled
us to himself, and given us the ministry
of reconciling others to God.

If you've been riding for any amount of time, you've likely drooled over the shiny new bikes on the showroom floors. We all like to dream of having the latest new bike, even though we probably couldn't afford it.

As born again Christians, we also know what it's like to have a brand new LIFE! I was radically saved out of a hard core biker lifestyle 40 years ago, and I have found this is not an uncommon story among Christian riders. I'm thinking our Father loves to move through radical conversions! Some of the worst sinners can become the biggest cheerleaders for God. "He who is forgiven much, loves much." (Luke 7:47)

The scripture today says that we have been given the ministry of reconciling others to God. He has placed this in our hearts with a nagging urge to share the good news. When we've been so radically changed and blessed, we just naturally want to share that with others. But even though we may want to share, those conversations don't always come naturally with unbelievers, do they?

One way we share our faith is just living our lives for the Lord. Our example will speak volumes. I've heard a saying that goes like this: "Preach the gospel at all times, and when necessary, use words." We can live in the world, without being 'of' the world. It means we have integrity about doing what is right and keeping our talk clean. We let our yes be yes, and our no mean no.

When conversations do come up about faith, I find it's easier to keep it about me. I talk about my personal experience and share about what a difference Christ has made in my life. The conversation eventually leads to how He can do the same for anyone.

We want to be ready to share our testimony when ever the opportunity arises. One pastor suggested we practice sharing a one minute testimony with a friend. So we're ready and know what to say when we get the chance to share.

We love to ride motorcycles, and it's an honor to be used by God in the things we love to do. Sometimes it's not even about the ride… it's about being available and being there for others to bring the Word into their life. You never know when He will speak through you to reach others.

Prayer Focus: Lord, help me to be ready to share when ever you need me to, whether it's by example or with my words.

New Roads

Matthew 7:13-14 NLT
The highway to hell is broad, and its gate is wide enough for all the multitudes who choose its easy way. But the Gateway to Life is small, and the road is narrow, and only a few ever find it.

Motorcycle enthusiasts are always looking for new roads to ride, and the twistier, the better. There's a road in Tennessee with 318 curves in 11 miles… better known as 'The Tail of the Dragon'. It's a bucket list ride for most riders, and it is a fun ride, but it's over in about 15 minutes.

Taking the road less travelled with Jesus, is a lot like the joy we find in riding a new road. It's a journey that takes us on many twists and turns as we learn and grow in our spirit-man. The interesting thing is that once we start on this path, it makes us hungry for more… like wanting to find new roads to ride, our spirit wants to go deeper into knowing God.

Sometimes the notion that God chose me and that I somehow found the narrow road to Jesus that few ever find, kinda blows me away. Who are we that God would adopt us as His own?

The truth is, He wants everyone to find Him and be saved, but He allows us to seek and find Him and make that decision ourselves. I mean who wants a relationship with someone who is forced to be with us, right? I may never understand the dilemma in knowing He 'chooses' us, but at the same time, it's our choice to follow. God's ways are so above my ways, I accept that I cannot figure it all out. But the scripture from Matthew today talks about how easy it is to miss Him in the wide easy highway of life. So how do we point people to the narrow road that leads to Jesus, when they have to make this decision on their own? There's a saying that goes: "You can lead a horse to water, but you can't make them drink."

I think a fun strategy is to use the FOMO effect (fear of missing out). When unbelievers see that what we have is rich, fulfilling, and blessed, and how satisfied we are living for the Lord, they will want it for themselves. It will become obvious that they are missing some of that in their lives, and will want what we have.

I'm not saying life is a bowl of cherries for a Christian, but **statistics do show that we are happier, live longer and have longer successful marriages.** How do we do it? With a little help from our God. Honestly, I don't know how people get through life without Him. I certainly wouldn't want to live without His love, provision and protection. What if we lived in such a way that others become envious? What a simple strategy, right? Just love the Lord, love others and love life! "All you need is love!" (Beatles)

Prayer Focus: Help me to live in such a way that others see You in me and want what I have.

A Sacred Trust

1

Corinthians 9:16-17 NLT
Yet preaching the Good News is not something I can boast
about. I am compelled by God to do it. How terrible
for me if I didn't preach the Good News!
...But I have no choice, for God has given me this sacred trust.

Motorcycle ministries are practically everywhere you see bikers. These riders have a special call on their lives and feel compelled to share Jesus with the culture. They help riders in practical ways, like helping bikers on the side of the road, visiting injured bikers in the hospital, sponsoring biker breakfasts and doing bike blessings. They do it because they know our God loves bikers too. Generally, bikers are not going to relate to a preacher man in a suit and tie, so God uses Christian bikers to show them He'll meet them right where they are. When they've seen our love for them, they've seen His love for them.

Not every Christian rider wants to be in a ministry group or club, and it's not for everybody. But if you have a heart to serve Christ with your motorcycle, this might be the place for you. Of course you don't have to be in a club or ministry to share your faith with bikers, but I find that being with a group of like-minded people on the same mission, empowers me to do more ministry.

The cool thing about Christian motorcycle ministries and clubs is that we all love the Lord and have a kindred spirit toward each other. We all serve on the same mission field, and we are family, no matter what patch we might wear (or not wear). People can see God just by seeing our love for one another.

Whether you ride with a ministry or are an independent rider, we all have the same sacred trust to share the Good News.

If you're not actively being a light for Jesus in the motorcycle community in your area, I challenge you to consider what your part is, and start each ride with a prayer about how you might make a difference. We all have our part to play in the body of Christ.

"Work with enthusiasm, as though you were working for the Lord rather than for people. Remember that the Lord will reward each one of us for the good we do…" Ephesians 6:7-8

Prayer Focus: Show me what my part is in reaching the motorcycle culture for you Lord.

Mind-sets

Romans 8:5-6 TPT
Those who are motivated by the flesh only pursue what benefits themselves. But those who live by the impulses of the Holy Spirit are motivated to pursue spiritual realities. For the mind-set of the flesh is death, but the mind-set controlled by the Spirit finds life and peace.

The mind-set of the biker definitely has it's own culture. We generally don't care about fitting into the norms of society. Some call it rebellion, but we tend to think of it as non-conformity. And we're in good company… **Jesus didn't conform to the religious society that He came from either.** He actually blew their thinking out of the water! He was so radical, they plotted to assassinate him, and succeeded. But little did they know, God had a plan to use this plot to offer the world a way out of dead religion. It's through what Jesus did that we find real life. Their dirty plot didn't end a radical movement… it started a revolution that still exists today!

The Christian biker is today's continuing radical message to the world… We follow the great non-conforming Savior! It's not about living to please the ways of the world. It's about finding the life giver that gives us the freedom to just be His, and this is enough. It doesn't matter if the world understands. When we have this kind of attitude, people notice.

So how do we "live by the impulses of the Holy Spirit"? It's when we listen to our conscience and know when to be there, and when to bow out of a situation to keep our integrity intact. We need to have discernment about when it's ok to hang out with unbelievers, and when it's not. "Bad company corrupts good character." (1Cor15:33)

People tried to condemn Jesus for hanging out with sinners. He set them straight when he explained that it's the sick people that need a doctor. But it takes a strong and mature faith to be able to hang out with unbelievers and not get sucked into their world. I personally had to take a 10 year break from that world and strengthen myself in the Lord before I was ready to go back into it as a missionary. Be real with yourself about where you're at in your walk before deciding to dive into ministry. Find an accountability partner to keep you straight. This is another reason I find being part of a ministry team helps keep me in line. We are accountable to each other.

If we are not sensitive to our integrity when it comes to our Christian walk in front of the very people we want to bring truth to, we lose our testimony, and they see us as a phony that doesn't "walk the talk". It can undo everything you've worked for in earning the right to speak into their lives.

Prayer Focus: Holy Spirit, make me painfully aware of your impulses to do the right thing and have discernment about walking with integrity so I don't lose any ground with those in my circle of influence.

Stories From The Road

Chappi's Story

No Longer Strangers

On a bright summer day, riding the winding roads through the Rocky Mountains in Montana, I watched God again at work.

The sun was glistening though the trees as each bend in the road displayed another spectacular view. Just before reaching the dam, we pulled off the road to take in the view. As we all lined our motorcycles in a row mine was the one on the end. I mention that because I normally ride in the middle so when we stop my bike is usually parked in the middle of the group. I didn't notice at the time but looking back, I see this little detail was all part of His plan.

As we walked to the overlook, I noticed 3 people sitting on a bench, engrossed in their conversation. I silently slipped by. One stopped me to say, "I noticed your bike - its beautiful". I looked over at my motorcycle. With the sun beaming on the tanks it appeared to have a golden glimmer adding depth to the dark brown paint. I thanked him and began to move on when he stopped me. "Can I ask you a question?" "Sure", I said. "What exactly is a Chaplain? Were you in the military?" I politely responded, "No, I was not in the military, I am a community Chaplain." **Suddenly the door to the kingdom was opened** and we walked through together along with the 2 others sitting on the bench. Our conversation led into a deep discussion of the Lord Jesus and how I had come to be a community Chaplain.

My motorcycle carries a brass coin of Jesus on the center of the tanks as well as a cross painted on the back fender. These items on my motorcycle along with a Chaplain emblem on the windshield has started the best conversations with many people as we ride through our beautiful country.

I have known for many years that God will use any passion we have to show Himself through His children to His other children that may have strayed or are lost. When those moments happen, He amazes me every time.

When the heart is willing to say, "Here I am Lord", He is willing to show up when you least expect it.

We simply stopped to witness His spectacular artwork. Then nature and man came together, and through His grace, a short and meaningful conversation took place that linked the 4 of us together forever.

Gentle Leaders

Hebrews 5:2 NLT
...deal gently with ignorant and wayward people, because we are subject to the same weaknesses. (paraphrased)

To see a brother find the miracle of a new life in Christ is the best. Many of us know what it's like to be radically changed. Did we come to Jesus because someone was beating us over the head with the scriptures, or telling us we're going to hell if we don't find Jesus? Generally, people are turned off by that approach. As the passage in Hebrews above says, the best technique is to deal gently with people who don't know our Lord.

We don't have to be ordained to share our faith, but we do need to be mature. Spending time in the Word, talking to God and continuing to meet with fellow believers is how we grow into maturity. The fifth chapter of Hebrews talks about becoming mature before we begin teaching others about spiritual things, and to not put ourselves in that honorable position just because we want it. We need to take time to know the Father so well, that we are sensitive to what His Spirit is saying to us about how and when to minister to others. He gives us nudges and promptings in our heart to share His love with others, and the beginning of understanding that is to spend time praying for and about the opportunities in our sphere of influence. Prayer should not always be a one-way conversation either… we need to listen for what He would say to us as well. Verse 7 of this chapter talks about how God hears our prayers because of our deep reverence for Him. It always starts with building ourselves up in the Lord.

There's a balance to this, as we also don't want to sit on the side lines all our lives either! Later in this chapter, Paul reprimands the people in verse 12 saying they had been believers so long, they should be teaching others, but they were still feeding themselves on the milk of the Word instead of growing strong with the 'meat' of the word. I would encourage you to dig a little deeper into spiritual things. Seek out spiritual gifts, and lean into everything the Lord offers His children. Chapter 6 of Hebrews tells us to 'move forward with further understanding'. **We need to move beyond the basic things of salvation, and get all the tools we can for the mission field.**

Because you're reading this, you are already dedicating time to spend with Him, and this is good. I would also suggest reading a chapter (or more as the Spirit leads) of the Bible each day as well, if you aren't already. God's Word is so rich! It teaches me something new every day. Things I read last year take on new meaning this year, so it never gets old, because God's Word is alive!

Prayer Focus: Speak to me through your Word and by your Spirit, and prepare me to teach others gently.

Set Apart

But you are God's chosen treasure - priests who are kings, a spiritual nation set apart as God's devoted ones. He called you out of darkness to experience his marvelous light, and now he claims you as his very own.

Being part of the motorcycle culture, we are in a group we can relate to and belong to. There's a camaraderie amongst bikers that brings us together with common interests and many levels of brotherhood in sharing our love of motorcycles.

Add to that the kindred spirit felt among believers, and you have an even stronger bond. Being part of the family of God is an amazing experience that can bring a stranger closer than a brother in an instant. **We've all been adopted by a Father that makes each one of us feel like His 'favorite kid'.** We come from all sorts of backgrounds and walks of life, but sharing the 'blood covenant' relationship with our Lord Jesus that sets us apart from the rest of the world, is an undeniable bond, even when there is nothing else we may have in common. It's a good feeling to be part of something so much bigger than ourselves, and I love sharing with others that **there's always room for one more, or that their place at the table is still available if they've been away and want to return.**

I had an amazing opportunity years ago, to encourage a back-slidden believer at a big annual motorcycle event. This was back in the day when motorcycle events were all about bikers coming together to roast a pig in the ground, have fun bike games, party and camp out. It was all good fun until the local 1% club came rolling in. The president of this local chapter and I had met before, and I was lucky enough the first time to escape his reach. But there he was again, and I found myself in an uncomfortable situation. Women are so vulnerable in the biker world, so if you are a woman, I highly recommend hanging with a few big brothers at these events.

In the course of trying to avoid this man, I actually caught the eye of the Regional P of this club who outranked the local president. An older hardened man who had great respect from his members. He came over to sit with me, and I thought for sure I was doomed for something horrible. To my surprise, he turned out to be my guardian angel that night, and sat with me the whole time, protecting me from the approach of others. We talked about a lot of things that night, and of course, my walk with Jesus came up. He shared that he was a believer, but had gotten so entrenched in the biker underworld that it was too late for him. He felt there was no way out, but I told him that nothing was too hard for God. If he really wanted out, he should privately start asking God to show him the way, and then not be afraid to walk through the door when it opened. I wasn't expecting any radical changes any time soon with this man, but from then on we had a very special private bond that no one else knew about, and I believe the **hope within him was renewed that night.** Oh, and no one in his club ever bothered me after that!

Prayer focus: Help me to be ready to share my faith with even the most hardened and unlikely people you bring into my life.

Equipped & Prepared

2nd Timothy 3:17 NLT
God uses [scripture] to prepare and equip
His people to do every good work.

The World is full of distractions that want to pull us away from the call God puts in our hearts to follow and serve Him. And yes, we also have an enemy that purposefully tries to trip us up, but there is a way to confront these things and stay on track. The Word of God has been given to us to equip and prepare us to fight these battles.

As a believer, you already know **the Holy Bible is a fascinating and amazing book.** It inspires me every time I read it. We can read it again and again, and get a different message speaking to us personally. We can never get enough of the Word.

In Paul's second letter to Timothy, he makes a point about how important scriptures are. He tells Timothy the Word will teach him what is true, and how to understand right & wrong, and that it will correct him when he's wrong. Paul told Timothy that scripture would equip him [and every believer] to do his missionary work.

Timothy was on a mission, and so are we. Our first responsibility is to keep ourselves on track to be effective in our mission field by staying in the Word. And like Timothy, we need to be ready to share the word of God whether the time is favorable or not. We are to patiently correct, rebuke and encourage people with good teaching when ever the opportunity arises. People today are looking for teachers to tell them whatever their itching ears want to hear. They will reject truth and chase after myths so that they can follow their own desires. (Chapter 4) That's why it's so important for us to know the Word and have a clear mind to speak the truth in every situation.

Remember, we're dealing with bikers here. We may be the only church they have ever been exposed to. They're not going to hear the Word from a pulpit (at least not at first). They're going to hear it from us. If they have questions, you want to be prepared to give good answers. We may not have all the answers, but we should know enough to give an accurate and truthful response. These conversations are the best timing to invite them to come to church or bible study with you to learn more. It's really nice to have a home study group going on that would welcome guests just for this reason. Most people will be more receptive to come to your home, than to step into a church setting.

Prayer Focus: Give me a hunger for your Word Lord, so I can be equipped and prepared for the mission field.

Expressing Truth

Ephesians 4:14 & 15 TPT
...And we will not be easily shaken by trouble, or led astray by novel teachings... instead we will remain strong and always sincere in our love as we express the truth.

The world is full of false teachings and cults, and we need to have discernment about what is truth and what is a lie. Sometimes the enemy will bring clever lies that sound right, but are meant to deceive. He is a sly one... going around like a wolf in sheep's clothing.

We don't want to get into arguing about doctrine or every little detail of faith. I'm talking about the blatant things that go against God's Word. When people talk about God or Jesus in ways that don't line up, that's when the truth in us can shine. In fact, part of our calling is to **shine like beacons of light in the darkness.** We don't hide our lights, we shine into those dark places, and it exposes the lies. Just like a flashlight exposes the dark corners in a room.

One day a lady said to me, "I'm a good person, I believe I'm going to heaven." So I am compelled to ask the obvious question: "Have you accepted Jesus as your Savior? Because it's not really about how good of a person you are. Murderers can go to heaven if they repent and accept Jesus!" This led to an interesting conversation, and I tried to gently and lovingly share the truth without it becoming an argument. I try to end these conversations before they get heated by concluding that we have different opinions, and offering to have a cup of coffee sometime to share more about it. Or even invite people to my bible study to learn more. If they have seen your 'walk' and have respect for you, they just might take you up on that, thinking you probably know something they don't. I love to leave them curious enough to want to find out more. It may be the way God is going to soften their hearts enough to listen.

When I hear people expressing a belief in something that is skewed about God or Jesus, **I see that as an opportunity to bring my light to the conversation.** It's easy to let it go and just think inside our heads that that person is very confused. It takes a bit of courage to open our mouths and share a truth. But we need to do it in an unthreatening way, and not let it become a debate. That is one of the sly ways the enemy will try to bring devisions, so be aware!

If you know enough of the Word, you can easily discern when something is not lining up with it. Unbelievers - or people who don't have the Holy Spirit revealing these things - don't generally take the Bible as absolute truth the way we do, so don't be too surprised if they don't accept our words. You may just be planting a seed of truth in their spirit that will one day grow.

Prayer Focus: Give me discernment and courage to share the truth when I hear things that don't align with your Word.

Blessing Bikers

2 Cor 9:8-10 NIV
God is able to bless you abundantly, so that in all things
at all times, having all that you need, you will
abound in every good work.

Blessing a riders bike is something pretty well received by even the most agnostic person. I guess the unbelievers figure, it can't hurt, right? It's a well accepted tradition, and it's like a 'freebie' opportunity for us to do ministry. So we need to make the most of these special days. If you get the chance to participate in doing a bike blessing event, it's a great way to get started doing ministry.

As believers, most of us ask for blessings before every ride. My husband has a wall sign in the garage that says, "Pray First, Then Ride". If you aren't already doing this, I highly recommend it. We aren't just praying for our safety, but asking for the Lord to give us opportunities to do ministry.

Stepping out in doing ministry among our peers can be intimidating, but I want to encourage you with today's scripture. God can bless us so we have everything we need to do His work.

The exact wording says He is able to bless us ABUNDANTLY so that **in EVERY situation, at ALL times, we have everything we need.** If we really believe that, then it's only a matter of us leaning into it. Here's some great scriptures to encourage you for this purpose:

1 Peter 3:15 (NIV) Always be prepared to give an answer to everyone who asks you to give the reason for the hope that you have. But do this with gentleness and respect…

2 Cor 5:2 (NIV) We are therefore Christ's ambassadors, as though God was making his appeal through us.

Mark 16:15 (NIV) …go into all the world and preach the gospel to all creation.

John 13:34 (NIV) …Love one another. As I have loved you, so you must love one another. By this everyone will know that you are my disciples…

Romans 1:16 (NIV) For I am not ashamed of the gospel, because it is the power of God that brings salvation to everyone who believes.

2 Timothy 4:2 (NIV) Preach the word; be prepared in season and out of season.

Acts 4:31 (NIV) After they prayed, the place were they were meeting was shaken. And they were all filled with the Holy Spirit and spoke the word of God Boldly.

Prayer Focus: help me to lean into the truth that you have given me everything I need to speak the word of God with gentleness, respect, love and boldness.

Stories From The Road
Bubba's Story

Interestingly, I have told this story many times to many people....but it never stops amazing me how our Father uses even those of us who don't have a clue what He is doing.

When my wife and I got married I bought my 1st Harley. It was a 1980 Harley Davidson Superglide - weird shaped tank, odd gauge cluster - but I loved that shovelhead motor. I was in the Air Force, and when I pulled into base housing with those 2" drag pipes, everyone knew I was home!!

Fast forward a couple of years and I had gotten out of the service, moved home and was working on my local police force. Kim and I were riding with a couple of other Christian couples and one of them invited all of us to go on a motorcycle camp out in the mountains of Arkansas. We were all going to stay in the same tent, and it was a Christian Rally. I was very excited. Well... we got there, and it rained all night in the tent. I was miserable. I did not really connect with the speakers, or the music either. Everybody there looked like me - white, middle class, basically all the same, except one. Over on the other side of the pavilion was a guy with hair all the way down his back with full sleeves of tattoos, looking out of place, and a little lost.

The Holy Spirit said, "Go talk to him." That began an argument that lasted several minutes in my head, with THE ONE WHO WILL ALWAYS WIN. (Read Jonah if you have any questions.) I gave up, walked over and asked him where he was from. He said the was from 3 states over, and had driven over 1000 miles to be there. Small talk continues until finally I asked him his "story" (everyone has one or one in the making). He said that while he was in prison he had been led to the Lord by some people who rode with this ministry, and he had been out of prison for a short time. He had come to the rally with those same people. Then, I asked him, "How can I pray for you? I feel like I am supposed to talk to you and pray for you." The young man said, "Man, I was a drug dealer, the police busted in my house in the middle of the night to serve a warrant, and I shot one of them. I thought they were robbers and they were there to steal my dope! I would have never, ever shot a policeman if I had known." He was obviously upset, his

head down, with a heaviness that I could see and feel all over him. Then he explained that he had tried to make contact with the officer that was shot, to tell him how sorry he was, and that he did not mean to do it, but the officer would not see him.

Then a light came on in my spirit, and I knew why - out of all the people that were at that rally - this young man needed my prayer. When I am off duty I never wear anything to look like I am in law enforcement. No one there but the people I was with knew what I did for a living.

I was able to look in that young man's eyes and tell him, "God sent me to you today to forgive you, as someone who wears the same badge, has the same job and understands the God who forgives." As I began to pray, chains were broken. Literally you could see him getting free from the guilt, shame, regret and come into the understanding that God wanted to deliver him - so much so, He sent a representative law enforcement officer who understands forgiveness by the amazing grace of our Savior. When we were done, we hugged and I walked away.

Don't ever doubt that the Holy Spirit is hovering over the earth looking for someone to be HIS representation of love. Since that day it has happened in stores, gas stations, jail cells, police cars, and court house lawns. Obey the Spirit! Offer the gift of HOPE, and HIS HELP and the eternal HOME that we all are searching for.

Ride hard, pray hard, show up, suit up and get into the game. The Lord is depending on you!

Kickstands Up

2 Timothy 2:21 NIV
If you keep yourself pure, you will be a special utensil for
honorable use. Your life will be clean, and you will be ready
for the Master to use you for every good work.

Kickstands up! The planned departure time for heading out on a group ride. Before this moment arrives, we get ready… we fill our gas tanks and empty our bladders. We do a quick safety check on the bike. We get our leathers, gloves and helmet on. We hear about the ride plan and mount our machines. Engines start, and we are ready. Kickstands push up, and off we go.

We can (and should) **do some preparation to be ready spiritually for the ride** as well. Are you prayed up? Do you have your testimony ready? How about having a bible and/or some literature for your church in your saddlebag? Do you have a card with your contact info to hand out to anyone you might pray for? How about a bike blessing sticker or coin? Does all that sound like overkill?

I admit, I'm a die-hard planner and organizer. These are gifts God gave me, so please bear with me for a minute, and think about how nice it will be, to be prepared for anything God may bring your way. Preparing is being a good steward and shows you take serious the call to minister with your motorcycle. It says that you are leaning into and expecting God to open doors of opportunity to share your faith. Are you ready to go in and 'possess the land' God may bring into your sphere of influence?

The prophet Joshua was leading the Israelites into the promise land. God taught him how to be a planner, and I love that! One day **God told Joshua to "get ready"** and get the people ready to cross the Jordan River into the land He was about to give them. (Joshua 1:2) Then three days before they were to begin the journey across the Jordan, God again tells Joshua, "Get your provisions ready." (Joshua 1:11) Later he told Joshua to "get ready" and build an altar. (Josh 22:26) Joshua was to be prepared in many ways to lead people.

Paul tells us that we should take it seriously when God gives us leadership. (Romans 12:8) The motorcycle culture is a mission field, and you are in a leadership role in this field! So there you have it! I highly recommend being prepared for doing ministry on the road.

Prayer Focus: Show me how to be prepared to do motorcycle ministry for every opportunity You bring.

Shiny Chrome Reflections

Prov 27:19 NLT
As a face is reflected in water,
so the heart reflects the real person.

Most of us love chrome on our motorcycles. We polish it until we can see our own reflection, and clean our bikes to look their best before going out. We add fancy accessories, new paint jobs, pin striping, etc., to make it unique and beautiful. We want to look good, and I think that's important, as long as it doesn't become our 'idol'. A clean beautiful bike will make a good impression, especially if we are representing our Lord.

Our lives should be a reflection of Gods goodness in the world, but it's sometimes hard to reflect a perfect God, when our lives are full of ripples and distortions, right?

It's always my prayer that people will see God in me, but when I'm having a bad day, I hope no one is looking. It's like Paul says - I do what I don't want to do... and I blow up my testimony before others. It truly saddens me when that happens! The best we can do when we blow it, is to admit it to those affected by it, and apologize or otherwise try to make it right. People we love need us to be 'real' and own up to our shortcomings, and not just pretend like that didn't happen. And non-believers need to know; **we aren't perfect, we're just forgiven!** "Hey Bro, I'm sorry about all that bad talk the other day… I was just frustrated and let it get away from me. God is not done with me yet. What you're seeing right here is a work in progress!"

Sometimes we need to forgive ourselves too. I admit, I hang on to that feeling of 'not good enough' for too long, and it hurts nobody but me! We can get stuck in that rut of feeling like a failure, and need to pull ourselves out and remember who we are to our Father. I find it helps to remember all the imperfect people in the Bible that God used in spite of their failures. My husband always says, "God doesn't call the qualified, He qualifies the called!" I always say, "I'm not where I need to be, but thank God I'm not where I used to be!"

Let's give ourselves a break and not beat ourselves up too much. Our Father knows we make mistakes, and He is willing to work with us to turn those bad days into building our character and integrity, if we let Him. He gives beauty for ashes.

Prayer Focus: help me to release any bad feelings to You and be a mirror to reflect your goodness and love.

White Wall Tires

Hebrews 9:14 NLT
How much more then, will the blood of Christ,... cleanse our
consciences from acts that lead to death, so that we
may serve the living God!

For me, there is nothing sweeter than the classic look of a 61' Panhead with white wall tires. The white wall tires make it look extra clean. There's something special about an antique classic bike with all the original parts & pieces. It all just feels right when we can see the bike as it came off the showroom floor.

Along the same lines, **nothing feels better than having a clean conscience.** Wikipedia explains conscience: *"In common terms, conscience is often described as leading to feelings of remorse when a person commits an act that conflicts with their moral values."* So it makes sense that if we have no conflicts with our moral/ biblical values, we will have a clean conscience, which is very freeing.

Conversely, there is such a thing as a 'seared' conscience where you feel no remorse about immoral things. Paul talked about it in his first letter to Timothy, speaking about how people living in the end times (many believe we are living in this time) would follow deceptive spirits and teachings that come from demons. He said those people had dead 'seared' consciences.

When we are dealing with worldly people, we have to keep in mind that they can have a dead conscience and won't care one way or the other about what is right or wrong. But here's the thing… their conscience might be burned, but we all have the truth dwelling in the depths of our hearts. It's our job to touch that part of their hearts, to begin the process of softening a hardened heart.

There can be different reasons for a hardened heart, and according to neuroscience, it may be a coping mechanism to repress bad memories, dull the pain of a distressful past, to the point where a person can be divested of caring about anything. So how do we soften a hardened heart? According to a scientific study*, a heart can only be softened with the cultivation of safe and caring attachments to others. They say healthy relationships are the antidote to facing too much separation and wounding.

So loving relationships can reach those who are distant and hurting in the world? **This is ministry we can do.** Everybody has a story, and building relationships with people is the way we earn the right to be heard and to hear their stories, which can bring healing and softening of their hearts. It means investing ourselves in other people, and asking about their story. They just want somebody to care enough to ask, and we know that there is no more loving relationship to point them to, than the love of our heavenly Father and His son Jesus.

Prayer Focus: Show me how to be a caring friend to the hurting people in the world. Help me to share my own story and be healed as well.

* *https://neufeldinstitute.org/softening-the-hardened-heart/*

Celebrating Life and Death

John 5:24 NLT
I tell you the truth, those who listen to my message, and
believe in God who sent me, have eternal life...
they have already passed from death into life.

One of the harder things we do as Christian bikers, is attend funerals and memorials for downed bikers. We show respect for the person and surviving family/friends by taking time to attend and participate. We can also **help people saying goodbye to loved ones** by supporting them afterwards. It's one of those times when almost everyone allows and even expects ministry to happen, and it gives us all pause to think about what comes next. Believers know exactly what comes next, but others will have questions and doubts.

Some of us, as Chaplains, are asked to perform ceremonies and memorial services, and what an honor and blessing to be part of that. Especially if it was someone you knew and loved. When it's another believer, we can really celebrate their life and know they are celebrating too, in their heavenly homecoming.

In this life, we are "constantly in danger of death" (2 Cor 4:11), but "we never give up, because even though our bodies are dying, our spirits are being renewed every day." (vs 4:16)

I know this is a 'mind bender' for unbelievers, but it's eternal security for us. There are many people that do have a half-baked belief in some sort of 'heaven', even if they can't define it. It's in losing a loved one that **they really want to put some faith in heaven**, to know that their loved one's are in a better place. What we have that they don't, is a living hope in eternity. "God himself has prepared us for this, and as a guarantee, he has given us His Holy Spirit." (1 Cor 5:5) This is the key thing to knowing that you know there is a God and there is a heaven being prepared for us - the gift of the Holy Spirit dwelling in us makes it real.

How do we explain this to people who don't have the Holy Spirit to make it real for them? In these moments where life meets death, and the questions arise, these moments are where we can try to have the answers. It's not an easy dialog, but the scriptures above help. Read the rest of chapter 5 for more information about what it's like to pass from death to eternal life. Ultimately, we will stand before God and be judged.... Unless we have Jesus to stand in for us. We are made right with God through Christ.

Knowing when to share this is a delicate matter, but we want to be prepared with some truth for when these questions come up. The best part of the story is that we can have total confidence in what lies 'beyond', if we have accepted the sacrifice that Jesus made for us, and that is the good news.

**For this world is not our permanent home,
we are looking forward to a home yet to come.** *Heb 13:14*

Prayer Focus: Teach me how to honor and respect the passing of a life from this Earth, and how to comfort those left behind. Show me how to minister your truths in these situations.

Don't Look Back

Phil 3:13-14 NIV
But one thing I do: Forgetting what is behind and straining
toward what is ahead, I press on toward the goal to win the prize
for which God has called me heavenward in Christ Jesus.

Our lives consist of our past, our present and our future. Our past has led us to who we are and where we are in life now. And what we do now, is what dictates what our future will look like; the near future, and on into eternity!

It's obvious that **the Bible encourages us to let go of our past** and move on. It's too easy to get stuck in our past problems and habits, and sometimes I think the whole journey of walking with God is about taking our past 'baggage' captive, and working it out through our great counselor, the Holy Spirit. He changes us from the inside out.

Getting born again won't magically make our past mistakes and choices disappear, there is a process in letting it go. We need to recalibrate our lives and our thoughts daily to focus on what God has for our future. 2nd Corinthians chapter 4 says that "our present troubles are small and won't last very long (compared to eternity!). And because we have this hope of glory in heaven, we don't focus on the troubles we can see now. Rather we fix our gaze on things that cannot be seen. For the things we see now will soon be gone, but the things we cannot see will last forever" (vs 17-18).

In other words, we don't dwell on who we were or the problems of the past, because everything is new! The old life is gone, and a new life has begun. And we can't fully grasp our new life, when we are hanging on the the old one. It doesn't happen overnight, and we are all in different stages of the journey. This is one thing we need to clarify with unbelievers, who seem to think we're supposed to be perfect once we become Christians. Actually, it's this train of thought that keeps a lot of people from accepting Jesus, because they think they need to be perfect before they can come to Him. I found it comforting to learn that it's the exact opposite! God takes us just the way we are, when we come to Him with a sincere heart. In fact Jesus said it's not the clean healthy perfect people that need Him… it's the broken, sick and needy people that He seeks out.

The important thing is that we begin this journey, and we keep moving forward - letting go of more & more of our past and our past selves, in exchange for becoming more like Jesus. We are all at different stages, and that's ok. We were all new believers at one time, right? This is a truth that we can pass on to those who are intimidated about meeting Jesus or walking with Jesus. Just get on the road with Him, and let Him lead you the way you should go.

There's a saying that I've heard: "we can't live looking into the rear view mirror - that is behind us. We can only move forward by looking ahead."

Prayer Focus: Show me what I'm still holding on to from the past that hinders me from moving forward, and help me to let it go. Show me how to help others in taking a turn in a new direction to follow Jesus.

Stories From The Road
Jo's Story

Truly blessed, I was turning 62, and enjoying a particularly epic road trip with some good friends. As my group and I traveled the open road, I was keenly aware of the unmistakable feeling of freedom that accompanied me on this trip. As we rode mile after mile in various weather, including torrential rain, extreme wind, 100 degree temperatures, beautiful landscapes and lazy roads, **it was obvious that God was reaching out and talking to me in a new and significant way.** It was as if the time had come to cross a threshold and move forward to the next phase of this life-journey and yet, there was something very exciting and comforting about this whole adventure that brought a lot of life to mind. He was moving me closer to Him and I knew it. He was also showing me

His amazing, kind love by allowing me to experience His presence, protection and care doing something I loved so much!

Over the many years of working diligently, there was always a sense of "get it done". My level of energy, commitment, strong work ethic and discipline had served my children and me well. There were many years of working day in and day out in sales and marketing in fiercely competitive arenas that transformed me into a robot of work energy. Suddenly, on this particular cross-country ride, the time had come to change gears and begin a journey that was not the same as it had been. The God-given gypsy in me said "enough" about titles, career mode, competing for approval, **it's time to see what God really has in store for me and LIVE!** And so, after 30 years in "corporate" America, He gave me the courage, mental fortitude, physical ability and drive to walk in His leading without worrying about what others would say. The kids were grown and on their own, and He was giving me a sense of leading and freedom I had not experienced until this trip. I felt like Joseph, Jonah and Elisha all in one! Just knowing He was so present as I rode mile after mile and talking with Him through the trip was truly transformational. There was no question **the road ahead was going to be amazing and require me to put my complete trust in Him** although I wasn't quite sure why at the time.

Fast forward nine years…..and the road has been anything but "conventional" or "normal" by society's standards or even the people closest to me. There have been more examples of severe teaching than I ever thought possible and yet, each time a new adventure presents itself, **I check and double-check to make sure the Holy Spirit is my true Guide.** The constants include riding and walking with Him. Riding is more sporadic but walking with Him has intensified and is not only a daily behavior, but I know He has used me in ways that appear completely crazy to others (For example, moving to three different states and back again in a 3-year span). Through it all He has provided the resources to make the moves, the job to sustain me and a motorcycle to ride! He is truly my Abba Father, God Almighty, Kinsman Redeemer, Sustainer, Jehovah Rapha, Jehovah Jireh and Boaz.

Through it all, my love for God, family and motorcycles is still as strong as ever and I thank God each day for the hundreds of people He has allowed me to meet and who have influenced me to love Him more. It is a Ministry and an enormous blessing.

All Weather Riding

All riders will eventually have to deal with weather on the road. I have personally ridden in heat, cold, rain, sleet, hail and snow (along with a lot of perfectly beautiful sunny days!) **Riding in the elements is definitely a challenge, but we press through, don't we?**

In 2014, I got to fulfill one of my 'bucket list' items and ride my bike to Sturgis with my husband and two friends. The ride was incredible in so many ways, and turned out to be the most challenging foul weather riding I've ever done. On the way there, we were fighting incredibly strong winds through the whole state of Wyoming! Then we approached a big black cloud, with no way around… Yes, it was a very wet ride! The rain didn't stop there, as it poured cats & dogs every day we were in Sturgis. My favorite half helmet didn't offer a lot in that kind of weather. Each evening we were drying out gloves & leathers over the heater. On the way home from North Dakota, we found ourselves racing to reach our hotel room in Colorado with another big black cloud chasing us with thunder and lightning close on our tails. I think we had one nice day of riding on the first day of the trip! I'm glad I got to check that off my bucket list, but I don't think I need to do that again any time soon.

When it comes to riding, we push through a lot of tough conditions to complete the ride. We don't quit. We don't always have a choice when the storms present themselves.

Sometimes life brings us hard challenges we have to push through as well. When "walking the talk" becomes hard, we push through to keep our integrity. When our marriages become hard, we push through until we get back on track. When our jobs are hard, we don't walk out. I know living that out is much harder than just saying it, and I want to tell you that I'm proud of you for all the hard work. Maybe you don't hear that often enough, so I want you to know that 'great is your reward' for how you've persevered. I'm sure your Father is ready to tell you 'well done'. Can you picture that? Can you picture Papa God grabbing you up into a big hug and telling you he's proud of you too?

Maybe you didn't have that kind of relationship with your Dad, and if so it might be hard to envision that moment. That's true for me, and it's what actually drives me harder to please my heavenly Father. I know He loves me more than anyone ever has, and I can't wait to curl up in His arms and feel that love. If you are lucky enough to have a loving Dad on this planet, then you likely have no issues making your heavenly Father proud as well. Good on you! He loves your confidence in His love too. Either way, *we have a good, good Father, and we are loved by Him - it's who we are!* (Lyrics to a favorite song.)

Prayer Focus: Help me to be strong and not give up when things get hard. Thank you for reminding me how much You love me and are already proud of me.

Bitter Cold

James 1:3-4 NLT
But When your faith is tested, your endurance has a chance to grow. So let it grow, for when your endurance is fully developed, you will be complete, needing nothing.

Cold weather riding is the hardest for me. I remember one of the coldest rides of my riding career back in 2012, riding from Sacramento over the mountains to meet up with some friends in Reno to join them in a ride to an Oregon rally. We had to meet them early in the morning, so we had to head out from Sacramento about 5am. It was early June, so I never expected the below freezing temps up in the mountains. **It was 16 degrees and icy cold!** It was too early for anything to be open to stop and warm ourselves up, so I would stop every 10 miles or so and put my hands down around my motor to defrost them. Going through Tahoe, there was a Denny's that was open, and we stopped for some coffee. It took a good 20 minutes for me to stop shaking. I was chilled to the bone!

Another bitter cold many of us have experienced is the betrayal by a friend or family member. This has to be the deepest felt heart ache in the world. This kind of hurt can leave us resentful and harden our hearts toward others. How can we forgive what seems unforgivable? I have struggled with this myself, and I know it can tear you up for a long time. It's so much better to find peace with these issues and move past them. We can't let a root of bitterness grow in our heart. It keeps us from loving others the way God loves us.

I know that Jesus also felt the bite of betrayal when one of His 'inside circle' of followers turned against Him. **We have a brother that knows what we're going through, and can get us to the other side.** We need to surrender these people to Jesus and ask Him to take the bitterness from us so we can move on. These kind of tragedies feel like the hardest trials! It's not easy to hear what the Bible says about counting it all joy when we face these things (really?!), but I know and believe that God works everything toward our good, and nothing is wasted. (When you can, find and listen to "Surrender" - a song by Third Day to help you get your breakthrough.)

These trials will show that your faith is genuine. It is being tested as fire tests and purifies gold - though your faith is far more precious than mere gold. 1 Peter 1:7 NLT

When we can get past our own hurts, we can help others get past theirs. This is how the 'kingdom' works… we comfort others with the comfort we have been given.

Prayer Focus: Help me to surrender those who have hurt me, and give you the hurt and bitterness I may still be holding on to, so I can minister healing to others who are hurting.

Quick to Listen

James 1:19-21 NLT
Be quick to listen, slow to speak, and slow to get angry.
Human anger does not produce the righteousness
God desires. So get rid of it all...

Anger is an emotion that we all have, and I have often asked my Father why we even need it. It doesn't seem to do anyone any good, and yet **there is a righteous anger that motivates us to do good works**. Jesus showed this kind of anger when he turned the tables of the vendors at the temple. They had turned a place of worship into a marketplace.

By far the biggest challenge for me in this area is controlling my speech. It feels like something I've been working on for most of my life. As I've said before, I'm not where I need to be, but thank God I'm not where I used to be!

If you claim to be religious but don't control your tongue, you are fooling yourself, and your religion is worthless. James 1: 26 NLT

Ouch!

When doing motorcycle ministry, we really need to 'be quick to listen' as today's verse says. Especially when we hear people getting angry. If we don't have a handle on our own anger, we can get caught up in it. If you are around others starting an angry conversation, or feel your anger being stirred, it's best to do nothing but listen, walk away, or pray under your breath for wisdom for how to turn the conversation in a different direction. We are to be the peace makers. All it can take to ruin your witness is a couple angry words. The enemy would love that. Don't let it happen.

Get to know the triggers in yourself for anger, and immediately ask God to replace that anger with a spirit of peace. This is like a 'bait & switch' tactic. When the enemy baits us with anger, we switch it to peace!

Another tactic I've used to curb the angry beast is to hold a token of peace to get centered. It might be a special coin or trinket in your pocket that you can hold for a few seconds to remind you to hold on to your peace. Maybe you can find something meaningful to you for this purpose. How about giving a special token to someone dealing with this problem to help them hold onto their peace?

When ministering to others, **your peace and calm will bring a peaceful atmosphere onto the scene**. Remember that you carry the Holy Spirit within you, so let the fruit of the Spirit flow out from you. Love, joy, peace, patience, kindness, goodness, faithfulness gentleness and self control.

Prayer Focus: Show me how to be a peace maker and bring my peace and calm to heated conversations. Let your Spirit flow out of me to show love, joy and peace to others.

Honoring Every Child of God

Back in the day when I first started riding - in my 'pre-Jesus' days, I remember most bikers having a pretty heavy prejudice against riders of certain colors. I've never been prejudice myself, but back then it was uncool to love every rider the same. Much the same as it used to be a cardinal sin to ride a Japanese made motorcycle. We used to bash those bikes with sledge hammers at camp outs!

There are still some residual racial preferences out there in the motorcycle world, but for the most part, it's not as heavy as it used to be. I find it interesting that bikers, and **people in general, naturally tend to gather with like-minded people of same ethnicity.** There is nothing wrong with this, as long as we welcome everyone in. I think it's normal to be drawn to our native 'tribe', if you will, and celebrate the things that make our culture unique and special.

James chapter 2 gives us a pretty stern warning about being prejudice. 'Love your neighbor as yourself' he says. 'But if you favor some people over others, you are committing a sin.' He even goes on to say this sin is the same as murder or adultery… sin is sin. 'Make no mistake, we will be judged by the same rules that we judge others', and 'there will be no mercy for those who have not shown mercy to others.'

As Christian's we can be an example of unconditional love for others, to those in our sphere of influence.

I love the kindred spirit that believers have for each other. The church I go to now has a very 'global' atmosphere, because we have people from all around the world coming to attend the schools of ministry and music that we offer. At any one time, we can have people from up to 70 different countries in a worship service! It feels really special to have this capsule of global believers in one place. You hear the different accents and see all the different skin colors. There is a definable glory and grace when we are all together worshiping the Lord with one mind and one Spirit.

I bought a t-shirt from a Christian motorcycle club years ago in support of them that says, 'Jesus Loves Bikers Too'. It's funny how parts of our society have a prejudice against bikers that has nothing to do with skin color. I remember a brother telling me about a conversation he had with a lady from his church. "Why do you wear all these leather clothes to church?" She asked, being offended by the attire. "Lady," he said, "I'm going to a biker event after church to do some ministry. Do you want to go to the event and try to reach those guys for Jesus?" Of course they don't. He went on to explain that bikers will relate to other bikers, and that Jesus loves bikers too. And Jesus was sending him to be His hands and feet to reach the people He loves.

Prayer Focus: Help me to be an example of unconditional love.

1st Peter 1:15 NLT
But now you must be holy in everything you do,
just as God who chose you is holy.

Be holy? How does a respectable biker do that and still be accepted in the culture? Let's look at what the Bible says about it.

First, I think it's kind of ironic that Peter is teaching on this; after all, he was the one who denied Jesus three times. That doesn't sound real 'holy' to me! But obviously Peter learned his lesson and has something to say about it. In vs 13, Peter starts by saying we need to exercise self-control. Next he says we should put all our hope in Jesus for our salvation. **He says to live obediently, and not slip back into our old ways of living to satisfy our desires.** We didn't know better then, but now we have the deposit of His Holy Spirit and belong to God, so we don't have excuses. As His children, we must be holy in everything we do, just as God who chose us is holy.

He goes on to tell us that we must live in reverent fear of God during our time here as temporary residents. God paid dearly to save us from the empty lives we had, and destined us for an eternity in His presence. Not with gold or silver, but with the precious blood of His son. God chose Jesus as OUR ransom long before the world began.

Did you get that? This is how much our Creator loves us. He chose Jesus to save us before the Earth was even made! Jesus was destined to die for God's treasured creation. You and me. Jesus was chosen for a specific destiny, and so are we. Our Father is preparing a place for us - His chosen from this creation - to live with Him forever. I sometimes wonder what He saw in me to choose me for this high honor. **We are a royal priesthood, a chosen generation**, destined for glory. I don't know about you, but this motivates me to want to live a holy life.

So back to living this out in front of the motorcycle culture. Our authenticity about being a 'Holy Ghost Powered, 100% Faith Driven' Christian will get their respect. It's when we don't live up to being holy, that they start seeing us as phonies and want nothing to do with what we profess. **We just need to be real and consistent in our walk with God before others.** We can't compromise anything that could effect our testimony. It's everything.

Prayer Focus: I am 100% committed to be authentic and holy to represent You as best I can in front of those you bring across my path.

Stories From The Road
OESD (Old English Sheep Dog)'s Story

While out riding, there are always opportunities to share my faith. **Just being available no matter where we are is where God can move.**

For example; on one road trip, my wife and I were headed for a rally in Colorado and had stopped for the night in Gallup, New Mexico. When we came out the next morning, my bike had a hard time starting and when it did start, it would not run well at all. It finally got to the point that we had to cancel our ride, rent a trailer for my bike and head for home. My frustration level was pretty high because we had been looking forward to this rally for some time. Questions come up like, "Lord, couldn't you have shown me this problem while we were at home so I could fix it before we headed out on this trip?"

We had a lot of fun (not!) finding a truck and trailer in that little cowboy town, but we finally did, after a lot more frustration and a big hit to our credit card account. So we were back in the hotel parking lot to load up the bike, when a Native American man came up to us, asking for money. We could tell he had been drinking, and had been in a fight just a few minutes earlier. He was quite angry with the world. Talking more with him, we learned that he seemed to fight with almost any one he met. This man was stretching my frustration level about as far as it could go. I was not in the mood for a fight!

Then my wife gave me 'the look', and it hit me. **My frustration was distracting me from seeing this as a divine appointment.** I took a breath and shook it off. I told him I didn't have any money to spare, but offered to pray for him. I was thinking, this should get this guy moving on pretty quickly.

But as we were praying, something unexpected happened. We could feel the presence of the Holy Spirit beginning to move on his heart. He started crying, and saying how he knew this was a wake up call, and that he needed to return to the Lord. He shared that he also felt the Spirit moving and felt that a weight had been lifted from him. He felt that the Lord was giving him a breakthrough with his anger. Through tears, he said he knew he needed to get off the beer train and get back with God. Wow. I gave thanks to the Lord for that and then we went our separate ways.

We finished loading the bike and began our trip home, but we were suddenly feeling much lighter. The whole encounter had a real authentic feel to it. We continued to pray for that man, hoping his breakthrough would stick, and that he would be able to touch many others in his world that saw the change in him. We came to feel that the 'half way to the rally' trip was worth it, if only to help this man get his breakthrough. **In fact that might have been the whole plan. God works in mysterious ways.**

Encounters With God

Mark 13:11 NLT
Just say what God tells you at that time, for it is not you
*who will be speaking, but the **Holy Spirit**.*

We don't need to do any of this ministry alone. **The Holy Spirit is our helper and our counselor.** He gives us the power to speak for God, to minister for God, and to discern spirits. He can open doors for us to work that we couldn't do on our own. A deep study on the person of the Holy Spirit will take you to a new level in motorcycle ministry. Without Him we can feel like we are doing everything in our own power, and that will only take us so far.

There are many ways to bring an encounter with God into the motorcycle scene, and the first prerequisite is to have an open heart to invite the Holy Spirit into your conversations, into your riding, and into your chance meetings. I mentioned earlier about getting 'prayed up' before you go out into ministry, but I will also be praying over every detail as it comes up out in the field.

For example, at a motorcycle rally or event where there are a lot of people, I'll pray that the Holy Spirit would direct my steps to the people He would have me interact with. Then when I am beginning a conversation with someone, I might ask Holy Spirit to be in the midst of the conversation and reveal anything that needs ministry that the person would be open to (in my thoughts, not out loud). If I ask if I can pray for someone, I will begin the prayer (out loud) by asking Holy Spirit to touch the person as only He can, to let them know God sees them, and hears their prayers. Then go on to voice their needs, all the time consciously trying to be a vessel for the Holy Spirit to speak through like it says in our scripture from Mark today.

It's amazing what can happen when we actually invite and expect the Holy Spirit to be present. It's also freeing for me, because I am essentially asking for His power to do ministry, and not trying to do it all on my own.

I know that Holy Spirit ministry is not a common thing in some church circles, so I hope you aren't too scared away by the thoughts in this devotional. If this kind of ministry isn't familiar to you, I again suggest that deeper study on the person of the Holy Spirit so He isn't a stranger. We can use all the help we can get in this ministry! Encounters with God happen when He shows up, and He shows up with we invite Him.

Prayer Focus: Help me to be aware of, and invite your presence in every encounter I have to do ministry.

A Place to Belong

Today's scripture is particularly special to me, going back to 2010 when I was in a particularly bad slump. The slump was really what launched me back into riding, and riding for Jesus. I needed a distraction from the depression that was creeping into my life.

I was enjoying as much 'wind therapy' as I could get, but riding alone gets… well, lonely. So I asked someone at church if there were any other motorcycle riders they could help me connect with. The usher pointed to a man walking through the doors with patches, black leather, long hair, thick beard and cut off gloves. This man looked way too familiar with the past God had saved me out of. So I immediately asked the usher if there was someone else he could point me to. I just didn't want to get sucked into that lifestyle again. It was very funny that three different people pointed me to this man when I asked that question, so I finally said, "Ok Lord!", and went and introduced myself. Turns out he was part of a motorcycle ministry and invited me to their monthly biker breakfast at a local restaurant.

I really wasn't looking to get involved with motorcycle ministry, but after hanging out with this group for the next 9 months, I literally became a part of the 'family' and joined up with them. It was a gift from my Father - placing me in a family and giving me a place to do ministry.

I share all that to point out that **sometimes our ministry is to our own brothers & sisters that need a place to belong.** We all feel a certain camaraderie with our friends that ride, and especially with believers. It's a good feeling to not be alone in the world. In the course of doing ministry, you might think about reaching out to our brothers and sisters of faith to see if they need anything. Maybe it's just a friend to talk to, or someone to pray with them about life's issues. Ask Holy Spirit to show you who needs a friend, and be that friend.

Maybe it's you that needs a friend. In that case, I want you to take note about my story; that I saw the depression creeping in and did something about it. I reached out and God helped me get through by connecting me with other believers. I'm not saying you have to go join up with a patched ministry, but we've got to stay connected to the family of God by going to church and being part of something bigger than ourselves. As a rider, I highly recommend **wind therapy with other like minded riders. Don't isolate yourself** where the enemy of our souls can pick you off.

"Two people are better off than one, for they can help each other succeed. If one person falls, the other can reach out and help. But someone who falls alone is in real trouble." Ecc 4:9

Prayer Focus: Thank you Father for giving me a place to belong, and the ministry of helping others to feel they have a friend.

On a Mission

1st Corinthians 10:35 NLT
...whatever you do,
do it all for the glory of God.

Sometimes the mission for my husband is to pull out the bike to go for a ride, and get to the nearest Dairy Queen. One of his famous lines is, "Do you know how Bikers spell Stop? DQ!"

Seriously though, I wonder how many of us think of ourselves as missionaries? **Not all missionaries go to Africa.** Sometimes it seems like we do so much mission work outside our country, when there are still so many unsaved in our own backyard. I remember a motorcycle ministry rally I went to at a church one time, and they had a big banner over the doors as you were exiting that said, "You Are Now Entering The Mission Field". It stuck with me.

Now I don't think of myself as an evangelist, but I do believe we should take the 'great commission' seriously. We are just regular 'joes' but **we carry the light of Jesus with us everywhere we go.** Sharing our faith could be as simple as telling the grocery check out clerk, "Thank you, God Bless!" My husband loves to do this. It basically inserts a little God into the moment, and more often than not, the person will say, "Thank you! You too!". This little moment of glory sets a tone that instantly brightens the space you occupy. These little unexpected 'God Moments' do effect people, and it's something we can use in our motorcycle outings.

If you notice someone having a talent for customizing their bike with beautiful detail, you can say, "God has really given you a gift with this, hasn't he?"

If there's a woman (or a man for that matter) with beautiful hair, you can say, "You are really blessed with beautiful hair!" (Something for the ladies to share with other ladies.)

If it's a beautiful sunny day, we can say, "What perfect weather for our ride today! Thank you Lord!"

These may seem like silly things, but you subtly acknowledge God in the little things, and naturally make God a reality in our every day conversations. It gives non-believers a different perspective, and offers a non-threatening way for them to see a world where God does exist. Granted, some people will blow us off as Jesus freaks, and they might not even realize those seeds are settling into their minds and hearts for later contemplation.

The world is our mission field! Every little word out of our mouths make a difference.

Prayer Focus: May the words of my mouth and the meditation of my heart be pleasing in your sight, Lord, my Rock and my Redeemer. (Psalm 19:14 NLT)

Humble Yourselves

James 4:10 NLT
Humble yourselves before the Lord,
and He will life you up in honor.

Being humble used to be an idea that turned me off a bit. When I thought of a humble person, I would think about a sweet old grandma with a bun in her hair, in a floral cotton dress carrying a handbag and a bible. I couldn't help thinking that bikers are just not humble people! We are the adventurous brutes of the world! We go into the dark places to share the gospel where that grandma lady would never go.

But being humble doesn't mean being weak or meek. It's more about not being arrogant or thinking we can do everything ourselves and don't need God's help. Being humble means always being aware that we need God, and always giving Him the glory in every victory.

At the end of chapter 4 in the book of James, he gives an example of someone saying, "I'm going to do this or that." When we should be saying, "If it's the Lord's will, I will do this or that." What does that imply? That we are seeking God about every decision. That's what real humility is. James says that we shouldn't boast about everything WE are going to do. All that boasting about ourselves is evil! Let's boast about what God is doing in our lives! When we put Him first, we will be honored and lifted up! We don't honor and lift up ourselves. We do the hustle for God because we are His soldiers, but at the same time we give Him the glory for everything.

James also said, "Humble yourselves before God. Resist the devil, and he will flee from you. Come close to God, and God will come close to you." This passage is powerful when you think about it. Let's not forget we do have an enemy. I don't focus on this, and neither should you, but this passage indicates that we do have an enemy that we have to resist. When we feel the heavy cloud of oppression or a resistance to doing what is good, we can 'come close to God' in prayer, and the enemy will have to flee. It's all about keeping God front & center, and realizing He is the All Powerful that can open doors we can't. He can soften hearts, we don't. We only bring the Word, and it accomplishes what it is supposed to do. It is never about what we are doing. It's about what God is doing, and how we can help Him accomplish His plan in the Earth.

So am I saying we can't take credit for anything? Basically, yes. If we boast about our own accomplishments, we get the praise of men, and that is all the reward we will get. But if we boast about how God blessed us in our accomplishments, great is our reward in heaven. Which would you rather have?

Prayer Focus: help me to stay humble and keep the hard hustle for You going.

Love Each Other

John 13:34-35 NLT
Love each other. Just as I have loved you, you should love each
other. Your love for one another will prove to the world that you
are my disciples.

Most bikers already have a kind of love and respect for one another, just because we all belong to the same culture of the motorcycle lifestyle. So it's not a big stretch to think about loving bikers in general. But this scripture is talking more about loving other believers. It's our love and respect for each other as believers that will cause people to know we belong to God. There is something different about us, and it sets us apart from the rest of the world.

It's not just our love for each other that sets us apart. It's knowing how much our Father loves us as well. There is something about having an attitude that 'It is well with my soul', that is very revealing about our faith. We aren't perfect, but we are loved and forgiven. We are accepted just the way we are, and our God has a plan and a purpose for us. He adopted us as His own, and we walk in the confidence of having a loving Father.

If you don't feel that love and confidence today, why don't you pause here and just close your eyes for a moment to allow His love to wash over you. Take your time. Spread out your arms to receive His hug. Wait for it. There it is… His love is so big, so true, so good. It's this kind of love that we want to bring to the world. The love that moves us. The love that is so real and genuine that it can't be denied.

My final word here would be to bless you with the priestly blessing of Aaron:

May the Lord bless you
And protect you.

May the Lord smile on you
And be gracious to you.

May the Lord show you His favor
And give you His peace.

As you venture out onto the highways and byways, may the Lord's blessing always be with you, and may His smile and favor go with you, and may His love and peace be what people sense all about you. May the Holy Spirit direct your paths, your words, and your ministry.

Prayer Focus: Let your love flow through me Lord. May I represent you well.